Smoking

Smoking

Look for these and other books in the Lucent Overview series:

AIDS
Dealing with Death
Endangered Species
Garbage
Homeless Children
Smoking
Special Effects in the Movies
Vietnam

Smoking

by Lila Gano

LUCENT
B·O·O·K·S

LUCENT *Overview Series*

Library of Congress Cataloging-in-Publication Data

Gano, Lila, 1949-
  Smoking / by Lila Gano.
    p.   cm. — (Lucent overview series)
  Bibliography: p.
  Includes index.
  Summary: Discusses major issues relating to smoking, in-
cluding its relation to American culture, economy, and disease.
  ISBN 1-56006-103-0
  1. Tobacco habit—United States—Juvenile literature.
  2. Smoking-United States—Juvenile literature. [1. Smoking.]
  I. Title. II. Series.
  HV5760.G36   1989
  613.85—dc20   89-12650
                                                        CIP
                                                         AC

To my family, special friends, and Lobo.

Contents

CHAPTER ONE

The Smoking Story—Past and Present

Archaeologists think that inhabitants of the Americas have been smoking for at least a thousand years. The earliest signs of smoking were found in the jungles of southern Mexico. There a raised design carved in stone, called a bas-relief, pictured a priest blowing smoke through a pipe. This bas-relief is believed to have been carved between A.D. 600 and A.D. 900.

Tobacco was an important part of the New World's culture and economy. The New World consists of North, South, and Central America. The native residents of the Americas grew and traded tobacco. They made pipe from clay and cigarettes from reeds. These were used in religious rituals and festivals. Some native tribes believed that smoking tobacco kept away evil spirits. Others used pipe smoke to call forth the Great Spirit, their God, in ceremonies.

In the late 1400s, native residents of North America and nearby islands off the southeastern coast introduced early European explorers to tobacco and smoking. As Christopher Columbus cruised the Caribbean Sea south of Florida, islanders presented him with gifts of dried tobacco leaves. Unfamiliar with the sight of people inhaling smoke, Columbus's curious crew reported that the natives "drank smoke." They called these natives "Indians" because they mistakenly believed they had reached India via a new route.

To these early European explorers, smoking was an unknown and strange custom of the New World. People in France, Spain, Britain, and other countries of the Old World had never heard of inhaling burning tobacco. It was not until the mid-1500s that smoking appeared in the Old World.

A Frenchman named Jean Nicot was among the first to introduce the seeds of the tobacco plant to the Old World. Nicotine, the active ingredient in tobacco, was isolated about 250 years later and named after him. Nicotine is a drug that can cause addition. It is found only in the tobacco plant and is actually classified as a poison.

Tobacco and smoking received a chilly welcome in the Old World. Queen Elizabeth I of England was stunned when Sir Walter Raleigh smoked his pipe in her majestic presence. In 1604 King James I assumed the British throne and led a fight against smoking.

Tobacco in the American colonies

During the early 1600s, British settlers arrived in America. Though King James complained about smoking, tobacco was credited with helping his colonists provide for themselves in the New World. The British had made several attempts to establish a settlement on the James River in what was later to become the state of Virginia. Named in honor of King James, the settlement of Jamestown had been doomed to disaster from the beginning—until tobacco came upon the scene.

Efforts to set up a community in Jamestown had resulted in death and disappointment. Harsh winters and lack of food claimed the lives of over five hundred men, women, and children. Chances of setting up a thriving community in Jamestown seemed hopeless, and by 1610 settlers were ready to abandon Jamestown.

But John Rolfe, the young Englishman who later married the Indian princess Pocahontas, convinced the settlers to try once more. He realized that they needed a way to support themselves, and he knew there would be a big market for tobacco in Britain.

With Rolfe's help, a new and flavorful tobacco plant was successfully grown and harvested in Jamestown. London merchants liked the new brand and bought it. By 1615, Jamestown began to thrive. Tobacco farming brought stability and prosperity to the tiny settlement, and tobacco became the first cash crop of the New World.

But King James was not convinced that tobacco was a dependable source of income for his colonists on the James River. He believed that smoking was a passing fancy and that the demand would soon

A colonial tobacco farmer tends his crop. Tobacco was America's first cash crop. Growing and selling tobacco turned poverty into prosperity for Jamestown, an early English settlement in present day Virginia.

weaken. He urged colonists to plant other crops. To discourage them from relying totally on tobacco for income, he imposed heavy tariffs, or taxes, on their tobacco crops. King James tried to make tobacco less profitable for the colonists to grow and more expensive for the consumer to buy. But because tobacco use was well established and spreading by that time, these tariffs did not slow down production or demand.

In the colonies, tobacco grew to become king. Its realm spread to every settlement on the East Coast with mixed success. By the mid-1600s, wealthy tobacco growers had built large plantations that were later supported by slave labor. But tobacco farming robbed the soil of vital nutrients. Because of this, planters continually searched for new farmland. They pushed westward and expanded into what is now Kentucky, Tennessee, and Ohio. In a sense, the search for fresh soil in which to plant tobacco caused British land holdings to increase.

While tobacco farming spread in the New World, pipe smoking and snuff dipping spread throughout the Old World. (Snuff is finely ground tobacco that is sniffed through the nose or placed in the mouth to suck.) In Britain, tobacco was first promoted as a medication to treat a variety of ills. These included deadly smallpox and the common cold. As tobacco became more affordable, more and more people began to use it in its many forms for pleasure.

Churches and governments get involved

Reaction of established institutions to tobacco use was sometimes dramatic. Churches and the governments of many nations tried to prevent the spread of tobacco, using threats of severe punishment. In seventeenth-century Turkey, those unlucky pipe smokers who were caught by authorities had their pipes thrust up their noses. The church and the government of Russia forbade smoking, and violators were tortured. In China tobacco sellers faced death by decapitation—having their heads chopped off.

But pipe smokers, snuff dippers, and tobacco chewers prevailed. By the mid-1800s, pipe smoking was the most common form of tobacco use in the United States. Wealthier Americans adopted the fine art of snuff dipping from the French court, and cigar smoking became popular in the early 1800s. The cigarette was last to make its appearance. It made its way from Spain to England and finally to New York in the late 1800s.

Historians believe that cigarettes were first made in Spain from scraps of tobacco left over from rolling cigars. They were considered a poor person's smoke because they were made from leftovers. It was cheaper to roll bits of tobacco in papers than to buy handmade cigars.

Eventually cigarettes became big business. A London merchant named Philip Morris started manufacturing them from a Turkish-

A woman handrolls cigarettes for a tobacco company. Even the best handrollers could produce only four cigarettes per minute. But the invention of a cigarette-rolling machine in 1883 made mass production possible.

grown tobacco. Today the Philip Morris Company produces the Marlboro and Virginia Slims brands and has a large factory in Richmond, Virginia. Other companies have also built factories in Virginia, Kentucky, and North Carolina. The Duke Company of North Carolina has introduced several successful new brands made from cheaper tobacco. Directors of this company have worked to develop quicker, more efficient ways of producing cigarettes.

Up to the 1880s, cigarettes were still rolled by hand, a very slow process. A fair amount of skill was required to roll shredded tobacco into a compact cylinder and seal it properly. Even the most experienced workers could produce only four cigarettes per minute. But the Duke Company jumped on a new idea to change all that.

James Bonsack, a young man from Virginia, had patented a machine to mass-produce cigarettes. In 1883 the Duke Company purchased exclusive rights to use this machine. The machine could produce 120,000 cigarettes per day. With production time slashed, the company was able to make more cigarettes for less money. It passed on cost savings to its customers. A box of ten cigarettes was reduced to five cents, half the previous price. Not to be left behind, other companies soon developed their own mass-production techniques.

The first to market to women

The Duke Company's business know-how did not stop there. It was among the first to openly sell its products to a brand-new market—women. Few women smoked openly around the turn of the century. Those who did risked becoming the subjects of whispers and gossip. They were suspected of "having loose ways." Smoking was also rumored to cause women to sprout mustaches and become incapable of having children.

But companies worked hard to improve the cigarette's reputation and increase its appeal to women. A new "feminine" wrapper was introduced by the Duke Company. A glamorous French actress, Madame Rhea, became the trademark of Cameo brand cigarettes. Other companies introduced Pearl's Pets and Opera Puffs. Marlboros were proclaimed to be as "mild as May."

Many came to believe that cigarettes were too dainty and delicate for adult males to smoke. In 1894 *The New York Times* announced, "The cigarette is designed for boys and women." And indeed, many young men and women became cigarette smokers.

Male youth of America found cigarettes appealing for many reasons. They were cheaper and milder than cigars. Cigarettes lacked the sickening side effects of cigars. As an added bonus, youthful smokers were enticed by colorful cards included in packs of cigarettes. Several series of cards were produced on such topics as dangerous occupations, national flags, and actresses. These cards were collected and traded like baseball cards. Coupons were also available with the purchase of certain cigarette brands. The coupons could be redeemed for albums for mounting and displaying the cards.

The anti-smoking movement heats up

With more and more youth smoking, parents and educators became worried. They accused cigarettes of causing physical, mental, and moral decay among American youth. In 1983 New York school commissioner Charles Hubbell summed it up:

> Many and many a bright lad has had his will power weakened, his moral principle sapped, his nervous system wrecked, and his whole life spoiled before he is seventeen years old by the detestable cigarette. The 'cigarette fiend' in time becomes a liar and a thief. He will commit petty theft to feed his insatiable appetite for nicotine. He lies to parents, his teachers, and his best friend.

Public anger turned into action. Concerned citizens organized to pressure state and local lawmakers to control tobacco use and sales. By 1890 a serious and powerful anti-smoking movement erupted. It was led by a tireless crusader, Lucy Page Gaston. She had fought previously against alcohol as a member of the Women's Christian Temperance Union. Her new enemies were now tobacco and the tobacco companies.

Gaston's efforts led to tough anti-smoking laws in the Midwest, her home territory. She was deputized and given power to enforce anti-smoking laws in Chicago. As a result, she appeared in court over six hundred times to testify against tobacco dealers who sold their products to children.

Many states adopted strict anti-smoking laws. Some banned the sale of tobacco products to children. In Wisconsin and Nebraska, mere possession of cigarettes by anyone was illegal. Frantic tobacco merchants rushed to dispose of their inventories before the laws took effect. Some burned cigars and cigarettes in the streets.

By the First World War in 1917, the negative attitudes toward smoking began to fade. The public had grown tired of the anti-smoking crusades. Though well-intentioned, the crusaders had too often used exaggerated scare tactics. For example, dramatic stories of children dying from smoking appeared in the press. Unlike today, anti-smoker activists decades ago had little scientific evidence to back up their claims. Americans resented unproved attacks on a product that more men and women were beginning to enjoy.

During the First World War, cigarette demand increased. The YMCA and other organizations distributed cigarettes to U.S. soldiers overseas. General Pershing, head of the Army command in Europe, wired headquarters in Washington, ordering tons of tobacco for his troops on the European front.

By the end of the First World War, people were no longer greatly concerned with the moral and health issues of smoking. Returning veterans had new lives to build, families to raise, and jobs to find. Cigarette sales boomed, and anti-smoking laws were ignored. In 1924 the movement lost its most vocal spokesperson. Lucy Page Gaston died. She did not live to see the medical research that would later verify her beliefs about the harmful effects of tobacco.

During the decline of the anti-smoking movement, researchers became more interested in the study of tobacco. Some believed that nicotine was the ingredient that caused tobacco use to be habit-forming. Many more years of research and study finally confirmed these suspicions.

The 1950s to the 1980s

By the mid-1950s, medical researchers had found much more evidence that cigarettes could be harmful. Cigarette smoking was linked to lung cancer and other serious illnesses. The tobacco industry rose to meet these attacks.

First, tobacco companies set up the Tobacco Industry Research Committee (TIRC). Headed by a respected researcher, the goal of TIRC was to sponsor research into tobacco and health. The committee also informed the public of the results of this research.

Second, companies designed filters for cigarettes. The filters were supposed to trap tar and nicotine, thus making cigarettes safer. The public accepted these claims, and cigarette sales climbed. But Congressmen and -women continued to attack the industry. Many did not believe that filters made these products safe.

Third, The Tobacco Institute was established. This powerful organization declared that existing research did not really prove that tobacco was harmful. It pointed out flaws in studies that had cast a bad light on cigarettes. By helping support the campaigns of many members of Congress, The Tobacco Institute became a powerful force

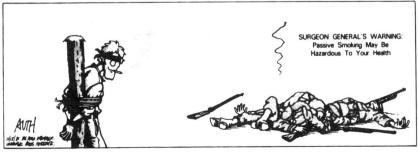

in Washington, D.C. The Tobacco Institute is a lobby—an organization that seeks to influence lawmakers, usually on behalf of its own interest.

Despite new medical discoveries of the 1950s, more and more Americans began smoking. By 1963 smoking reached a peak. About one-half of all adult men and one-third of women smoked. The government called it an epidemic.

Emphysema caused by tobacco use

Former Surgeon General Luther Terry released a study in 1964. Dr. Terry's report was not good news for the tobacco industry. It concluded that cigarette smoking was indeed a cause of lung cancer in men and was suspected to have a similar effect on women. The report also said that smoking increases a person's risk of dying from emphysema, a serious lung disease.

In the 1970s, public and medical interest shifted to the effects of cigarette smoking on the non-smoker. Involuntary, or passive smoking, became a big issue, particularly in the workplace. Passive smokers do not smoke. But they breathe in many of the harmful chemicals that drift off the end of a lit cigarette or are exhaled by a smoker.

U.S. Surgeon General C. Everett Koop declared war on smoking during the 1980s. Dr. Koop's office published studies stating that nicotine was an addictive drug and that passive smoking endangered nonsmokers' health.

A landmark report by former Surgeon General C. Everett Koop fueled the simmering fires. This report in 1986 confirmed that passive smoking can cause serious illness. Koop warned that children of smokers suffer more respiratory problems, from the common cold to pneumonia. ''Smokers have a responsibility to assure that their behavior does not jeopardize the health of others,'' Koop stated.

Dr. Koop stirred up the country again with a new report in 1988. He concluded that the nicotine contained in cigarettes caused people to become addicted to them.

Tobacco has played a significant role in this country's history. Antismoking crusaders have battled with tobacco producers and manufacturers for many years. They have fought their battles in the courts, in Congress, and in the media. Though volumes of medical evidence point to tobacco as a cause of serious disease, people still smoke.

CHAPTER TWO

The Modern Smoking Experience

In the United States today, over two million teenagers smoke cigarettes. They smoke at home, in their cars, at work, and with their friends. Most smoke because their friends or family members do.

Since 1975 researchers at the University of Michigan have studied smoking trends among young people. These studies show that smoking rates among young people have declined somewhat in recent years. About 18 percent of high school seniors smoke, a drop of about 7 percent from 1979. High school girls smoke slightly more than do boys. In college the gap widens. Young women are even more likely than men to smoke.

In their studies, researchers have discovered other facts about smoking. Sixteen percent of high school students in the Northwest smoke. The lowest rate is in the West, with only 7 percent. High school students who smoke generally have lower grades than non-smokers do, and those who plan to go to college are less likely to smoke. Regular smokers use more alcohol and illegal drugs. Researchers also discovered that about 53 percent of high school seniors who smoke half a pack or more daily have tried to quit and failed.

Smoking teens have plenty of company. Over fifty-one million adults also smoke. The average adult cigarette smoker uses about twenty cigarettes per day. The majority of adults who smoke started when they were young. Surprisingly, nine out of ten would like to give up their habit because they are worried about their health.

Smoking trends affected by education

Anti-smoking campaigns and education have affected smoking trends. Fewer adults smoke today than at any time since the 1950s. In 1964, 42 percent of the population smoked. About 27 percent still smokes today. The biggest decline has occurred among adult males. Two-thirds of the work force does not smoke. Many companies now actively discourage their employees from smoking.

Though Americans as a whole smoke less, some groups do smoke more than others. People with low educational levels smoke more than people with college degrees. Blue-collar workers, such as carpenters, smoke more than white-collar workers, such as accountants. The percentage of blacks who smoke is greater than the percentage of whites.

The American Cancer Society (ACS) is concerned about the number of women who smoke. In its pamphlet called *Facts and Figures*, the society states, "Although the percentage of women smokers is declining, in absolute numbers more women are smoking and smoking more than in the past, causing lung cancer rates to rise."

The federal government is also concerned about the health of smokers. Based on over thirty years of research, former Surgeon General Koop considered tobacco use a national health problem. The Department of Health and Human Services (HHS) oversees health and social programs including those sponsored by the Surgeon General's office. In an HHS publication called *Smoking, Tobacco, and Health*, the problem is defined. "Each year cigarette smoking causes the deaths of more than 300,000 Americans, principally from heart disease, cancer, and chronic obstructive lung disease. It can

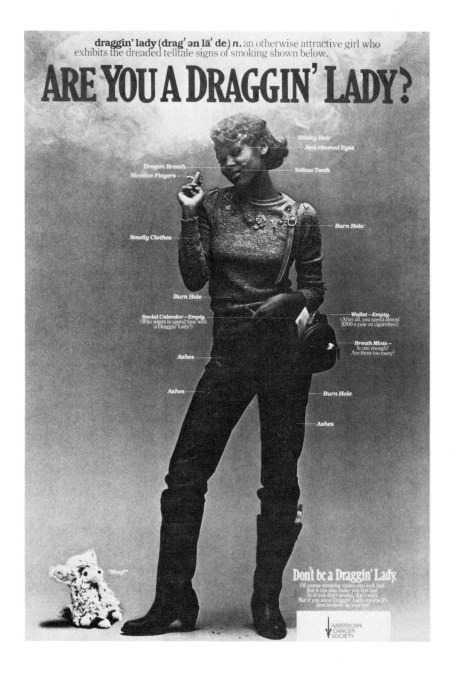

legitimately be termed the most devastating epidemic of disease and premature death this country has ever experienced.''

Americans are listening to these warnings. Forty-one million have stopped smoking. Most ex-smokers were unable to quit the first few times they tried because their addiction was so strong. Dr. Tracy Orleans helps smokers give up cigarettes. She states, ''The addictive process in smoking is no different from the addictive process with other substance abuse.'' The mind and body develop a strong craving for nicotine just as they do to alcohol or cocaine. Some medical experts claim that giving up drugs or alcohol may even be easier than giving up nicotine.

Though the number of ex-smokers is climbing, new members join the smoking club each day. About a million teenagers took up the habit in 1987. And a growing number of young men are using smokeless tobacco, including snuff, and chewing tobacco. Most teens who smoke or use tobacco products start before they are thirteen years old. There are many reasons why.

Why young people smoke

Young people smoke or use tobacco products for many reasons. The main one is because of peer pressure. Junior high is often where friends expose friends to tobacco products. A boy on the softball team offers his teammate a pinch of smokeless tobacco. A girl advises her best friend that smoking helps keep off unwanted pounds. Study partners light up to relax just before the big exam. If a non-smoker has friends who smoke or use tobacco, he or she will probably also be invited or urged to use it.

For some young people, smoking is a form of rebellion. Since most parents frown upon tobacco use, smoking is a way for young people to express independence from parental authority. Smoking can be one way to say, ''I am no longer a child. I can and will make my own decisions.'' Smoking makes adolescents feel more grown up.

Many young people smoke because they learn it from family

members. Smoking may be a family tradition. Smoking parents tend to raise children who will smoke. Seventy-five percent of teens who smoke have at least one parent who also smokes. Older brothers and sisters who smoke help set an example for young ones. Children learn by imitating people around them. It is ironic that most smoking parents object to their children using tobacco.

Young people smoke for other reasons, too. Some young smokers report that smoking relaxes them. Chemically speaking, however, nicotine is a stimulant. It speeds up bodily functions, like the heartbeat. Others claim that smoking puts them at ease in social situations and helps them cope with the stress of adolescence.

Young people smoke for a variety of reasons. Many claim it relaxes them and helps them cope with the stresses of growing up. Young women may smoke because they believe it keeps them thin and thus more attractive.

Some health officials believe that many young women smoke to help control their weight. Magazines, television, and the movies are filled with images of slender women. These role models set high physical standards that some young women try to meet. Dr. Donald Davis is Director of the Office on Smoking and Health (OSH) under the Office of the Surgeon General. He is concerned about this trend. ''Unfortunately, people don't realize that gaining an extra five or ten pounds, if people quit, is a much lower health concern than the increased risk from smoking,'' he said.

There are a variety of outside influences that affect a person's use of tobacco. In the end, to smoke or not to smoke remains a personal decision. But more and more people have decided that smoking is a fading fad.

CHAPTER THREE

Smoking and the Media

Cigarettes were used to help set the mood for romance in many old movies. Smoking in the moonlight brought two lovers together in the 1942 film *Now, Voyager*. In an award-winning performance, Bette Davis played the role of Charlotte, an unmarried woman controlled by her overprotective mother. Her leading man, Paul Henreid, played the part of Jerry, an unhappily married man. The condensed scene that follows takes place on a hotel balcony on a "velvet tropical night." There the main characters share a smoke and a moment of intimacy. This dialogue is paraphrased from this scene.

JERRY: Charlotte, there's no telling what wild feelings you might bring out in me. Cigarette?
(Charlotte takes one and he does too. In the matchlight their eyes meet. He offers her his lighted cigarette.)

JERRY: Why, darling, you're crying.

CHARLOTTE: They are only tears of gratitude. An old maid's gratitude for the crumbs offered. No one ever called me darling before.

JERRY: Please don't talk like that.
(Later in the scene, Jerry kisses Charlotte. She becomes limp and returns his kisses. The camera turns away and focuses on the cigarette in her hand. It falls to the floor as the scene fades.)

Cigarettes have accompanied many actresses and actors to stardom. Stars from the 1940s and 1950s often smoked in their films. Humphrey Bogart and Lana Turner puffed their way through romances, comedies, and dramatic stories. (Humphrey Bogart died of cancer of the esophagus when he was only forty-two years old.) Beautiful women seemed more glamorous waving a cigarette in front of the camera. Leading men seemed tougher and more manly. *Time* magazine summed this up in its April 18, 1988 issue:

> Without smoking, it seemed, great detectives could not detect, writers could not write, lovers could not languish, heroes were deflated, and vamps were declawed.

In the 1940s and 1950s, many celebrities approved of smoking and appeared in cigarette ads in magazines. Cigarettes were promoted on both radio and television until 1971. Perry Como, a popular singer, hosted his own show in the 1950s. He made many commercials for his cigarette sponsors. In one ad he said, ''Twenty little white cigarettes in a clean white pack, and they are very happy they grew up to be Chesterfields. And we are very happy too, because they are so wonderful for you.''

Government gets into the act

The evidence that cigarettes were not so ''wonderful for you'' that mounted in the 1950s prompted the tobacco industry to add filters to their cigarettes and to advertise their new filtered products heavily. L & M filtered cigarettes adopted the slogan, ''Just what the doctor ordered.'' ''More doctors smoke Camels than any other cigarette,'' announced the makers of that brand.

The government frowned upon claims that the new products were safer. Levels of tar and nicotine were stated in cigarette ads. These levels could not be easily checked, and claims were misleading. As a result, the government asked the tobacco industry to stop advertising levels of these ingredients. The tobacco industry complied.

Hollywood movie stars of the 1940s and 1950s made smoking appear glamorous and romantic. In this scene from the 1942 movie Now, Voyager, *Charlotte and Jerry (Bette Davis and Paul Heinreid) share a smoke in a moment of romantic intimacy.*

The government later reversed itself, and the ads resumed. In 1966 the industry and the government joined together to develop standardized tests for measuring tar and nicotine levels. The tests made it possible to compare levels of these substances accurately between brands. All ads now state the levels of tar and nicotine.

In the mid-1960s, the government did some "advertising" of its own. Congress required a label on each pack of cigarettes and in all advertisements stating that smoking was harmful. The message read, "Warning: The Surgeon General has determined that cigarette smoking may be hazardous to your health."

Congress went a step further in 1984. Companies were required to double the size of the warnings. The size of the printed letters and the box surrounding the print were made bigger. New, stronger wording was also required. The labels must be changed every few months to one of the following messages:
- Cigarette smoke contains carbon monoxide.
- Quitting smoking now greatly reduces serious risks to your health.
- Smoking causes lung cancer, heart disease, emphysema, and may complicate pregnancy.
- Smoking by pregnant women may result in fetal injury, premature birth, and low birth weight.

Responsible advertising, or just blowing more smoke?

During the 1960s, the tobacco industry changed some of its advertising approaches. Sensing public pressure, the industry stopped advertising in school and college publications. Product promotions on campuses were stopped. By 1964 the industry had adopted a code of ethics in its advertising. It volunteered to monitor itself. The code stated that advertising would not be designed to appeal to the young. Noted sports figures and teenage idols would no longer be used in ads. Models must be at least twenty-five years old and must appear that old. The industry asssured the public that ads would not depict smoking as an activity that increases success or sex appeal.

Pressured by Congress, the tobacco industry was pushed a step further to curb ads. Television and radio were recognized as having great advertising impact. Congress directed that all tobacco ads be removed from the airwaves in 1971.

The smoking ban affected the anti-smoking campaign as well as the tobacco industry. Before the ban, anti-smoking public service announcements were common on radio and television. When cigarette commercials left the air, so did many of these announcements.

Once the biggest advertisers on the airwaves, cigarette ads soon dominated the print media—newspapers, billboards, and magazines.

Tobacco companies spent vast sums of money to purchase space for their ads. In 1985 the industry spent over two billion dollars on advertisements. Cigarettes continue today to be among the most heavily advertised products in this country.

The struggle to limit tobacco advertising is far from over. The American Cancer Society and other health groups want a total ban on all cigarette ads. They do not want them to appear in any printed material. Congressional approval would be required for this to take effect.

The tobacco companies oppose a total advertising ban. They believe that their right to advertise is protected under the First Amendment, which guarantees all Americans the right to free speech. They maintain that ads are not designed to recruit new smokers, especially young people. The intention of the ads is merely to influence current smokers to change brands.

One tobacco company has taken steps to encourage young people not to smoke. The R.J.Reynolds Tobacco Company has placed advertisements in magazines that young people read, like *Teen* and *Seventeen.* The ads advise young readers not to smoke and to resist peer pressure to start. R.J. Reynolds further states that its product advertising "is not designed to make smokers out of non-smokers." Rather, the goal is to persuade "smokers of competitive products to switch to one of our brands."

The International Advertising Association defends the tobacco industry's right to advertise its products. This association studied the issue of tobacco ad bans in sixteen other countries. Their report states, "advertising bans have not been followed by significant changes in tobacco consumption. In fact, such consumption is still increasing in many countries years after a ban was introduced."

Advertising strategies

Selling is the name of the game. Companies with a product or service want to make it appealing to consumers. Ad agencies are often hired to help sell the product. They can create a product image and give it personality.

Certain brands of tobacco products have images that have become very well-known. The rugged, lonesome cowboy is a famous symbol for Marlboros. A camel, of course, represents Camel cigarettes. To update his image, the camel now wears sunglasses and a flight jacket and has a cigarette hanging from his lips. This new look is based on the leading character from the popular movie *Top Gun.* An attractive, slender woman is associated with Virginia Slims and Capri.

Other themes reappear in ads on a regular basis. Tobacco products are often associated with fresh air and outside activities. Models walk through the woods, splash around in a lake, or stroll on the beach while they smoke. Sometimes models participate in sports events or social gatherings with friends. The images often show positive people having fun. They are happy and relaxed, with broad smiles and white teeth. By law, the ads in magazines, newspapers, and billboards must state health warnings. These warnings are a sharp contrast to the bright, positive themes portrayed in the ads.

The American Lung Association (ALA) believes that cigarette ads are designed to appeal to viewers' emotions and not to their brains. Many other items, such as cars and beauty products, are also advertised to appeal to our emotions. These ads often convey subtle messages— that consumers will become more attractive, look younger, or be happier if they use the advertised product. Sometimes it is difficult to separate fact from fantasy in the advertising world.

In her book *Are You Ready to Quit Smoking?*, Linda Bryson writes about the realities of cigarette ads. ''Cheryl Tiegs, as well as many

These old cigarette ads from the 1950s are responding to people's fears that smoking may be unhealthy. They claim that smoking filtered cigarettes is safe.

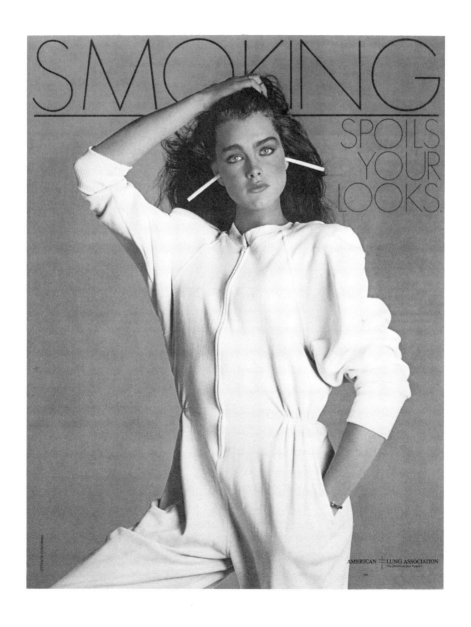

other models who advertised cigarettes, would not smoke themselves. Models would not look good in close-ups if they smoked. But in the meantime too many young women are imitating the models by taking up the habit that most models wouldn't consider.''

Film star and model Brooke Shields has this to say about smoking. ''Cigarettes—yuck! I think that smoking is disgusting in every way. In case you didn't know, here are some of the awful things that smoking does to your body: nicotine residue from cigarettes collects on your teeth and turns them brown; it causes bad breath and a hacking cough. Your hair smells and your clothes closet stinks.''

Besides expensive ads, tobacco companies use other methods to sell and promote their brands. Coupons that can be collected and turned in for gifts are an extra bonus for buying some brands. Free samples of products, such as smokeless tobacco, are offered through the mail.

Tobacco companies sponsor events

For more than a decade, tobacco companies have sponsored sports, music, and cultural events. They often give away free samples of their products at these events. The Virginia Slims Tennis Tournament has become world famous. It attracts top players. The Kool Jazz Festival and the Benson & Hedges Ice Skating Show are other examples. Marlboro cigarettes helped to support the rematch for the America's Cup sailboat races in 1988. The leader of the American team, Dennis Conner, wore a Marlboro and Pepsi patch on the front of his jacket as the television cameras rolled. The amount of money spent for events like these is estimated to be over forty million dollars annually.

The Tobacco Institute found another worthy cause to get involved in recently. It contributed money to the National Association of State Boards of Education (NASBE). This nonprofit firm accepts funding from outside sources but does not endorse their products. With the Institute's help, the NASBE put together two booklets—*Helping Youth Decide* and *Helping Youth Say No*. Both offer excellent guidance to

Annual Cigarette Consumption per Person

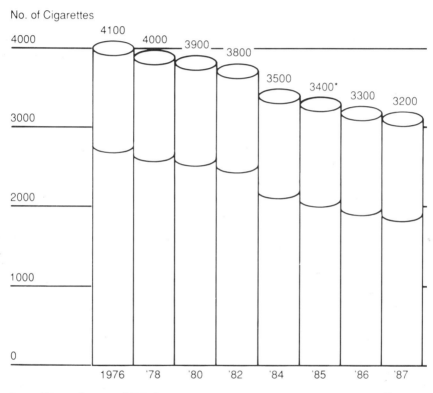

No. of Cigarettes

Source: Tobacco Situation U.S.D.A., Sept. 1985.   *Estimated

parents in understanding teenagers. The use of tobacco is briefly discussed, and developing good communication between parents and teens is stressed.

Critics question the real motive behind the partnership between NASBE and the tobacco industry. Some believe that the industry is trying to overcome a bad image by showing concern for the problems of young people. The industry is trying to develop a wholesome image, according to a report put out by the American Heart Association (AHA).

The tobacco industry's influence on the media

The tobacco industry may influence our lives in another way. Because of the large amount of money tobacco manufacturers spend for magazine and newspaper space, they may be able to pressure editors not to print articles that criticize smoking. Magazines and newspapers charge a lot of money for the full-page ads they sell to tobacco companies. Some editors report that they have lost profitable tobacco accounts after printing critical articles on smoking.

A report by the AHA provides evidence about the tobacco industry's influence on what we read. Some health writers claim that they have been told to avoid writing about smoking because their magazine was running cigarette ads that month. One writer claimed he was fired after he referred to the hazards of smoking while covering the Kool Jazz Festival.

Dependence on tobacco advertising, some argue, has caused editors and publishers to avoid or to tone down critical articles on smoking. The lack of coverage about this important health issue has resulted in less information and understanding about smoking. Some critics believe that this situation has led to higher smoking rates. Others question the morality of using money to influence the media.

CHAPTER FOUR

Tobacco and the Economy

The manufacture and sale of tobacco products is a multi-billion-dollar industry. In 1987 tobacco companies sold about thirty-two billion dollars worth of tobacco products, mostly cigarettes. After all their operational expenses were paid, their estimated profits were 6.4 billion dollars, an increase over 1986.

Profits are up because prices are up. A pack of cigarettes cost 1.25 dollars in 1988 compared to about eighty cents in 1981. Because fewer people now smoke, prices must rise to make up for the loss of revenue. According to the government, Americans bought about 574 billion cigarettes in 1987, down from 583.4 billion in 1986.

Though Americans are smoking less, tobacco is still one of the most important crops grown. This is because of the amount of money it earns per acre. At the market, tobacco brings higher profits than most other crops. In recent years, tobacco has earned over 3,000 dollars per acre per year before expenses are deducted. Most other crops sell for far less. For example, cotton earns about 460 dollars per acre, and wheat earns about 100 dollars per acre.

Farmers can earn big money growing and selling tobacco, compared to other crops. Many farmers grow it along with their other crops. Ninety-two percent of the total tobacco crop is grown in just six states: North Carolina, Kentucky, Georgia, South Carolina, Virginia, and Tennessee.

American tobacco is a plant that is related to the tomato, eggplant, pepper, and petunia. Tobacco plants grow from two to eight feet tall. Their large leaves are twelve to forty-two inches long and six to fifteen inches wide.

Different types of tobacco

Several different types of tobacco are produced from tobacco leaves—flue-cured, air-cured, including burley and Southern Maryland, and fire-cured. The flue-cured leaf is used in cigarettes and chewing tobacco. After harvesting, it is dried, or cured, by heat that is pumped into flues, or metal passageways through the curing barn. The temperature in the barn is controlled to rise gradually. Burley and Southern Maryland tobacco are also used in cigarettes and chewing tobacco. Instead of drying by heating, however, these varieties are cured naturally or air-cured in the sun and in open barns. Most cigar tobacco is air-cured. Fire-cured tobacco is used in snuff, chewing tobacco mixtures, and strong cigars. This variety of tobacco is cured by smoke from wood fires, a process similar to curing a ham.

After farmers harvest and cure their tobacco crops, they are usually auctioned off to a manufacturer. For over seventy years, six major tobacco companies have dominated the manufacturing business. These companies are Philip Morris, Inc.; R.J.Reynolds Industries; Batus, Inc. (Brown and Williamson); American Brands, Inc.; Grandmet USA (Liggett & Myers); and the Loewes Corporation (Lorillard).

The large profits from tobacco production have enabled these firms to buy companies that sell a variety of other products. Tobacco firms own companies that make cookies, beer, and cereal. For example, in 1985 the R.J. Reynolds Company bought Nabisco Brands, Inc. Nabisco makes such family favorites as Oreo cookies and Planter's peanuts. With this merger, the largest consumer product company

Farmhands called "pullers" arrange freshly picked tobacco leaves on a wagon before it is taken to the drying barns. The tobacco industry also provides markets for other types of businesses important to the economy. Tractor and fertilizer makers, trucking companies, and advertising firms all profit from tobacco.

in America was born, RJR Nabisco.

Tobacco farming and manufacturing are intricately linked to other important segments of the economy. Fertilizer manufacturers and tractor makers depend heavily on farmers, including tobacco farmers, to buy their products. Trucking and shipping firms make money distributing tobacco products. Grocery stores make a profit on each pack of cigarettes they sell. Almost one-half of all cigarettes are sold by grocery stores. In addition, each year tobacco companies spend roughly two billion dollars on advertising. They are among the most valued customers of advertising agencies, as well as magazine and newspaper publishers.

From seedling to store shelf, many workers are involved in bringing tobacco products to the consumer. Tobacco is estimated to be responsible for some two million jobs. The tobacco industry is quick to remind its critics of this important benefit to the economy.

In his article "The Cigarette Companies: How They Get Away with Murder," David Owen challenges the tobacco industry's claims about the jobs it provides. He further "credits" the tobacco industry with providing jobs to funeral directors and grave diggers who bury people who die of smoking-related illnesses. Owen points out that florists earn income from providing flowers for the funerals, and smokers help keep surgeons, firemen, and street sweepers employed.

Smokers who want to quit have fueled the fires for more new businesses. Private clinics, classes, and treatment programs to help people stop smoking have sprung up all over the country. Americans paid counselors and therapists an estimated 100 million dollars in 1988 to help them kick the habit.

Imports and exports

Tobacco trading in the international arena is also big business. The United States imports and exports more tobacco than any other country in the world.

In 1987 the U.S. imported nearly 711 million dollars worth of tobacco leaves and products. Imports are up an average of 7 percent since 1986. Foreign-grown tobacco leaves are desirable because they are generally cheaper than American-grown tobacco.

Turkey and Greece are among the largest suppliers of leaf tobacco. The leaf they export to the U.S. is called oriental tobacco. It is blended with American-grown tobacco to make cigarettes. Tobacco leaves are also imported from Brazil, Zimbabwe, India, Thailand, and other countries.

Besides importing leaves, the U.S. buys millions of foreign-made cigarettes and cigars each year. For the year 1987, the value of these manufactured imports was estimated to be 83.5 million dollars, up 10 percent from the previous year.

Because tobacco is used in every nation in the world, the market for U.S. tobacco leaves and products is large. Though more expensive than the tobacco of many countries, American tobacco is considered to be of higher quality. Tobacco quality depends a great deal upon when the leaf is harvested. It must be done at just the right time before the plant ripens too much. About one-third of all American tobacco is sold to other countries. The biggest customers include Japan, Europe, Australia, and Egypt.

Quantities of exported tobacco products, especially cigarettes, are also up. From 1986 to 1987, the number of American cigarettes sold abroad increased by 36 percent. Over 100.2 billion cigarettes were exported to 109 nations in 1987. Most of these went to Japan, Belgium, Hong Kong, and Saudi Arabia, according to The Tobacco Institute. The export of such large amounts of tobacco has brought mixed reactions. Certainly, the American economy benefits from selling products abroad. The U.S. sold more tobacco than it bought in 1987. This means that the economy experienced a positive balance of payments for tobacco. That is, more money came into the country than left the country for tobacco trading.

Exporting illness

But some critics accuse the industry of exporting the hazards of serious illness to make money. Many countries do not require health warning labels on cigarettes imported from the United States. Smokers in other countries may not be aware of the medical findings that link tobacco use to many illnesses.

A consultant to the World Health Organization, Mr. Gregory Connolly, is worried about cigarettes that are sold without warning labels. In an interview with ''Face the Nation'' in 1988, he spoke out on this issue. He said that in America, labels warn pregnant women that smoking may hurt their babies. The same cigarettes sold in another country may say nothing about possible dangers to unborn babies. Instead, the same pack sold overseas may be labeled only "Quality Choice."

Mr. Connolly also discussed levels of tar and nicotine. He pointed out that even though a pack of American cigarettes sold abroad may be labeled "light," it may contain twice as much tar and nicotine as the same "light" brand sold in the States.

A tobacco farmer checks on the progress of tobacco leaves drying in an old-style flue-cured barn. U.S. tobacco exports are on the increase. But tobacco products sold in foreign countries often do not warn consumers of the health risks of smoking.

Cigarette taxes

Tobacco products are among the most heavily taxed items sold in America. Roughly one-third of the total price of a pack of cigarettes goes to pay taxes to state, local, and federal governments. Sales and excise taxes totaled over 11.2 billion dollars for 1987. (An excise tax is a tax placed on the manufacture, sale, or purchase of a specific product within the country.) Though state and local taxes vary, the federal government earns sixteen cents in excise taxes on every pack of cigarettes sold.

Governments at all levels benefit from tobacco sales. At the federal level, tobacco sales brought 4.8 billion dollars into the national treasury in 1987. Taxes on cigarettes earned 99 percent of this total. The remaining 1 percent came from the sale of chewing tobacco, cigars, and snuff. All states tax cigarettes, and over half tax cigars and other tobacco products. The states also earned about 4.8 billion dollars in the same year, mostly from cigarette sales. At the local level, 392 cities and counties tax tobacco products. In 1987 they collected close to 196.6 million dollars in revenue from tobacco sales, again mainly from cigarettes.

The tobacco industry has spoken out strongly against excise taxes on its products. It argues that the poor are unfairly taxed at the same rate as the rich. Low-income people pay the same amount of excise tax for a pack of cigarettes as do middle-and upper-income people. But because they earn less money, excise taxes take a bigger percentage of their income. Those who are blue-collar workers and who have less education also tend to smoke more than do the middle and upper classes.

Besides unfairly taxing lower-income people, the tobacco industry complains that excise taxes cause the economy as a whole to suffer. When prices of tobacco products go up, sales generally go down. If sales are low, farmers, producers, packagers, and distributors can lose jobs.

On the opposite side of the tobacco industry, several health organizations want to raise taxes on tobacco to discourage smoking. The American Heart Association, the American Cancer Society, and others support an excise tax increase from sixteen cents to thirty-two cents per cigarette per pack. They also encourage states to raise their sales taxes on tobacco products.

Health organizations argue that if Congress were to double the federal excise tax, the number of smoking teens and adults would drop significantly. Tobacco products would become too expensive for many people to continue the habit. The price tag would discourage others from ever taking it up.

The federal government—is it pro- or anti-tobacco?

The former Surgeon General and the federal government's senior health official, did not want people to smoke. Dr. C. Everett Koop worked closely with the Office on Smoking and Health (OSH) to get this message accross. Under the Department of Health and Human Services, he and the OSH prepared reports on the effects of tobacco use. They helped to educate the public about the consequences of smoking. Since 1980, the budget to operate the OSH has totaled over twenty million dollars. Taxpayers have paid for these efforts.

Ironically, taxpayers also pay for federal programs that support the tobacco industry. These programs were put in place to help tobacco farmers obtain reasonable prices for their crops. The price support and loan programs are managed by the Department of Agriculture (USDA).

The price support program is designed to limit tobacco production so that market prices remain stable. If too much tobacco were produced, the market would be flooded. When the supply of any product exceeds demand for it, prices go down, and farmers earn less money for the work they do. (Similar programs exist to maintain price levels for corn, rice, cotton, and peanuts.)

In addition to price control supports, the USDA also runs a loan program for tobacco farmers. When raw tobacco cannot be sold at

BLOOM COUNTY

market for a specific price, the USDA steps in to assist farmers. The department wants to prevent farmers from having to sell their crops below a certain level where they would lose money. To prevent farmers from selling at a loss, the department gives them a loan equal to the minimum price that was specified. This loan is taken in place of selling the crop to a tobacco manufacturer for processing. The government loans the farmers money to cover their living and business expenses. The tobacco is kept and sold later when the market price goes up again. The loans are repaid with interest at that time.

No crops means no money

Farming is a risky business. Bad weather can destroy a year's worth of work overnight. No crop means no money. When this happens, farmers may be unable to pay back their loans. The government also loses. Losses from tobacco loans have totaled over fifty-eight million dollars since this program went into effect about fifty years ago.

The Tobacco Industry Is a Profitable Business

Statistical Reporting Service, USDA

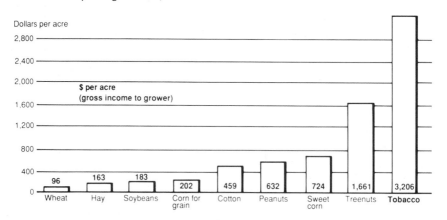

Dollars per acre

$ per acre
(gross income to grower)

96	163	183	202	459	632	724	1,661	3,206
Wheat	Hay	Soybeans	Corn for grain	Cotton	Peanuts	Sweet corn	Treenuts	Tobacco

Similar programs for other crops, such as corn and cotton, have far greater losses when compared to tobacco, however.

The USDA must pay for the administrative costs of the price support and loan programs for tobacco and other crops. Public pressure has reduced the money spent on these programs, but they are still costly. The same employees who chart market conditions for tobacco also figure them for other crops. Just how much labor is devoted to running tobacco programs alone has not been measured. Thus, the exact cost of operating tobacco programs cannot be precisely calculated. The total cost of running all of these programs for several crops, however, runs between fifteen and eighteen million dollars annually.

Production and sale of tobacco brings big money to the government and puts dollars in the pockets of many people associated with the tobacco industry. The powerful tobacco lobby in Washington, D.C., works to preserve the industry's right to conduct business. Because of the power of the tobacco industry and the support of large numbers of smokers, tobacco will no doubt remain deeply rooted in the present and future economy of the United States.

CHAPTER FIVE

Smoking and the Law

In 1984, in response to mounting concern over health hazards related to smoking, Congress passed the Comprehensive Smoking Education Act. This act provided for the health messages that appear on smokeless tobacco and chewing tobacco, as well as the increase in the size of warning labels that appear on packs of cigarettes and in cigarette advertisements.

The Comprehensive Smoking Education Act also established the Office on Smoking and Health. This office coordinates medical research and education under the Department of Health and Human Services (HHS). The smoking act also requires cigarette companies to report the chemicals used in tobacco processing. These reports must be submitted to HHS. HHS must find out if any of these chemicals are harmful and report their findings to Congress.

In 1988 the federal government clamped down on smokers traveling on airplanes. It banned smoking on flights within the United States that are less than two hours long. About 80 percent of all flights fall into this category. People who break this law can be fined up to one thousand dollars and will be "welcomed" by an FBI agent upon landing. Interfering with a smoke alarm in the restroom of a plane can also result in stiff penalties.

Though federal control over smoking and the tobacco industry has tightened, the government could do more. For example, some activists want the Food and Drug Administration (FDA) to regulate tobacco products. The FDA regulates items that are classified as foods, drugs, and cosmetics. However, the FDA does not consider tobacco to be a drug, even though it contains the drug nicotine.

Tobacco products are not considered drugs by the FDA for two reasons. First, they are not advertised as drugs by the manufacturers. Second, the FDA defines a drug as a product that is used for the specific purpose of changing body functions or treating illness. Tobacco firms generally make no health claims about their products.

Ironically, the FDA does regulate Nicorette, a gum that contains nicotine and is sold as an aid to quit smoking. Nicorette is considered a drug by the FDA because its intended use is to treat a medical problem—tobacco addiction. The reasoning used by the FDA to defend its position on the tobacco issue has been seriously questioned by critics.

State laws

Laws to control or prevent cigarette sales and smoking have been passed by many state and local governments. Over forty-two states and four hundred cities and towns limit smoking in public places such as city hall, stores, and elevators. Eleven states require restaurants to offer separate seating for non-smokers. Ten states have passed laws to control smoking in the workplace.

In response to this anti-smoking trend, The Tobacco Institute has generally fought against laws that limit smoking. In 1989 Horace R. Kornegay, president of the Institute, wrote:

> Those who consider smoking a menace, rather than an enjoyment, have acted as prosecutors, trying to convince the public they have an outright case. But isn't the jury entitled to some serious doubts?

Despite objections from the tobacco industry, Minnesota was the first state to enact a sweeping law to protect the non-smoker. In 1975 the Minnesota Clean Indoor Air Act was passed. This act made it illegal to smoke in all public places, unless an area was set aside specifically for smoking. Smoking is not allowed in city buses, grocery stores, offices, and many other locations. Minnesota's law is considered a model because it inspired other states to pass similar laws.

In 1980 voters in Florida and California had a chance to get tough with smokers. When all the ballots were counted, however, it turned out that voters had rejected a proposal to separate smokers from non-smokers in all public places. This was a victory for smokers and for the tobacco industry. The Tobacco Institute made this comment:

Diners react with indignation when a smoker lights up. Many states now have laws separating smokers from nonsmokers in public places like restaurants and office buildings. More and more nonsmokers are demanding smoke-free areas where they can avoid the dangers of passive smoking.

Clearly, most Californians and Floridians believe the individual respect, tolerance, and accommodation needed to resolve most everyday displeasures cannot be legislated. Mutual consideration is and must be the business of the people, not the government.

Since then, voters in both Florida and California have taken steps to limit smoking in selected locations. Florida does not allow smoking on trains and buses traveling through the state. California state law prohibits smoking in grocery stores, in health care centers, on public transportation, and in many other places as well.

California voters hit smokers in their pocketbooks in 1988. Voters passed a law called Proposition 99. It increased the state tax on cigarettes from ten cents to thirty-five cents per pack. The extra money raised from this tax will help pay for several state programs and services. Among these are health care for the poor, anti-smoking education, and research on tobacco-related disease.

The tobacco industry gets involved

The tobacco industry did not want Proposition 99 to pass. A tax increase would make cigarettes more expensive, and sales would decline. To help sway public opinion in its direction, the industry made television commercials that linked the passage of this bill to gang violence, discrimination against smokers, and more profits for doctors.

Ironically, the grandson of Mr. R.J.Reynolds, the businessman who had made fortunes for the tobacco company bearing his name, supported the increase. Mr. Patrick Reynolds blasted the industry's advertising. "They [the tobacco industry] will do anything to fool the voters of California." He added, "Most new smokers are kids, and kids are more price-sensitive than adults." Mr. Reynolds blamed cigarettes and chewing tobacco for killing his grandfather, mother, father, and two aunts. "I just don't want to see anyone else die," he said.

Besides taxing cigarettes, states use other methods to control sales and promotion. In Maine, teenagers no longer have unlimited access to cigarette vending machines. Utah does not allow cigarette advertising on billboards.

Local smoking laws

Dozens of communities, large and small, have taken action to control smoking. They have enacted local laws that limit smoking in public places. From New York City to Beverly Hills, California, cities and towns are moving toward reducing the number of places where smokers can light up.

In 1983 residents of San Francisco approved Proposition P. This law was designed to limit smoking in the workplace. It is one of the toughest city laws in the country, when it comes to smoking. The law requires all employers to prepare a written policy on the subject

"ON THE OTHER HAND, AT LEAST THEY DIDN'T BAN THE SMOKING SECTION COMPLETELY..."

of smoking. Under Proposition P, the rights of non-smokers prevail. If a non-smoker objects to smoke, the employer must find a solution that satisfies the non-smoker. Failing this, smoking can be totally banned in that particular work area.

Time reported a minor smokers' rebellion in its April 18, 1988 issue. When the city council of Beverly Hills banned all smoking in restaurants, business dropped by 30 percent. Restaurant owners panicked. The city council backed down and compromised. It decided to allow smoking in restaurants if enough ventilation was provided to clear the air.

New York City's Clean Indoor Air Act went into effect in April

1988. This law requires that half of all restaurant tables be reserved for non-smokers. About seventy city inspectors will check on the restaurants to make certain their owners obey the new law. Smoking restrictions also apply to stores, banks, offices, museums, and most other enclosed places.

In the April 18, 1988 issue of *Time*, the mayor of New York, Ed Koch, commented on the new law. "This is going to be one of the best self-enforced laws in the country. There is no one more enraged than a nonsmoker forced to breathe in secondhand smoke." Enforcement of most smoking restrictions has relied mostly on social pressure and voluntary compliance.

Tobacco takes on the courts

The battles over health and smoking have spilled over into the courts. Since 1954, over three hundred lawsuits have been filed against tobacco companies. For the most part, these suits claim that smoking caused death or illness. The cost of fighting these legal battles has been extremely high for the tobacco industry.

Some observers believe that tobacco companies have spent between 600 million and 3 billion dollars to defend themselves in the courtroom. This expensive effort has paid off for them. Thus far, only one jury has ruled against a tobacco company.

The courts have generally held that smokers have been warned about the hazards of smoking since 1966 (the year when warning labels first appeared on cigarette packages). People who smoked after that time had been duly warned of the danger. They assume the risks and responsibility themselves, according to several court rulings. Prior to 1966, however, there were no warnings. Tobacco companies were not necessarily protected from responsibility for their products.

On June 13, 1988, a jury found a tobacco company partially responsible for the death of a smoker, Rose Cipollone. This was the first time in history that a tobacco company was held accountable for harm done to a user of tobacco products. A federal court ordered the Liggett

Group, makers of Chesterfields and L&M, to pay Cipollone's husband 400 thousand dollars in damages.

Mrs. Cipollone had smoked one pack of cigarettes a day between 1942 and 1968. She smoked Chesterfields and L&M prior to 1966 because she believed their ads. The ads suggested that the products were safe. Chesterfield's slogan was "Play Safe: Smoke Chesterfields." L&M was advertised as "Just what the doctor ordered."

The jury ruled that the ads were misleading. At the time they were run, medical research already indicated that smoking was a health hazard.

Despite this setback, the tobacco industry remains confident about

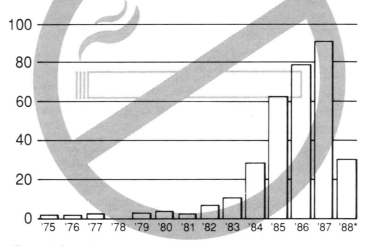

Number of Smoking Bans Decreasing

The number of laws that ban smoking in workplaces, restaurants, stores, and enclosed public places.

*Through August

Source: Americans for Nonsmoker's Rights

its legal position. Josiah Murry, an attorney for the Liggett Group, stated to the *Los Angeles Times*, ''We do not consider we lost the case.'' Chairman of Philip Morris, Maxwell Hamish, commented, ''There is nothing about the verdict that indicates a break in the dike. One case does not make a trend.''

Some observers disagree. They believe that this case is just the beginning of more court rulings against tobacco companies. Famed attorney Melvin Belli said to *USA Today*, ''We are going to file suits from Anchorage to Miami, from Portland, Maine, to San Diego. We have been moving slowly over the years, but this one will make the rest easy.''

The world takes up arms against tobacco

Tobacco has tangled with the governments of nations throughout the world. Anti-smoking laws in other countries have focused on limiting ads, requiring warning labels, and controlling the use of tobacco products. According to the American Cancer Society, over thirty-seven countries require warnings on packs of cigarettes, but most do not.

France passed a Smoking Prevention Law in 1976. Smoking in schools, hospitals, and on public transportation was banned. Smoking in elevators and in places where food is served was also made illegal. In France, tobacco companies cannot advertise in publications that young people read.

Sweden has one of the most ambitious anti-smoking movements. In 1973 a national campaign to eliminate smoking was launched by the government. The major goal of the campaign is to prevent children born after 1974 from becoming smokers. Another goal is to use education and peer pressure to reduce the total amount of tobacco that Swedes use.

To help achieve the goals of this anti-smoking campaign, the Swedish government passed some strong laws. Health warnings about the hazards of smoking are required on tobacco products. Carbon

monoxide, tar, and nicotine levels must be stated on products, as well. The government has also limited the size of ads that appear on billboards.

From large countries to small ones like Sudan in Northern Africa, governments have passed laws to control tobacco use. In 1982 all cigarette and tobacco advertising was outlawed in Sudan. Smoking in closed public places, such as meeting rooms, was also forbidden.

A serious anti-smoking movement came to life in the 1970s and 1980s. Non-smokers and health groups organized and pushed for laws to limit tobacco sales and smoking. Their voices have been heard by local, state, and federal officials. Judging by the strength of the anti-smoking movement, a bumpy road lies ahead for the tobacco industry.

CHAPTER SIX

Diseases Linked to Smoking

> The suicide was an open and shut case. "Death was sudden
> . . . in ill health for some time," read the tactful obituary. But
> the dean's family and friends knew that his life had been
> destroyed by his pathological addiction to nicotine—that his habit
> had become a form of suicide, and that he had blown off the
> top of his head when the agony of smoker's emphysema had
> become too much to bear.
> "Nicotine: Profile of Peril"
> By S.S. Field, *Reader's Digest*
> September 1973

Former Surgeon General Koop and other health experts blame tobacco use, mainly cigarettes, for more than 300 thousand early deaths each year. The average American can expect to live for about seventy-five years. If people did not smoke, many believe they would have a greater chance of living longer and healthier lives. More people die from illnesses linked to smoking than from AIDS, highway accidents, or heroin overdoses combined.

A lit cigarette produces smoke— a mix of gases and tiny particles. Cigarette smoke contains thousands of chemicals. The American Lung Association (ALA) lists several substances in smoke that have been shown to cause cancer in lab animals. After smoke travels through the mouth, 70-90 percent of these chemicals stay in the lungs. The most active substances in smoke are nicotine, tar, and carbon monoxide.

Nicotine is a natural poison found only in tobacco leaves. It is used to make some medicines and insecticides. New smokers may feel nauseous from nicotine intake. Tolerance builds quickly, though, and their bodies soon learn to accept this drug. But not without a price.

The nicotine from just one cigarette causes an increase in heart rate, reduces blood circulation, and lowers skin temperature. It enters the bloodstream in seconds. At first, nicotine stimulates the brain and central nervous system. Later, though, it depresses these systems. Because nicotine constricts blood vessels, the heart must work harder to pump blood faster. This puts extra stress on the heart muscle.

Former Surgeon General Koop issued a major report on nicotine in 1988. It was called *The Health Consequences of Smoking—Nicotine Addiction*. It states that cigarettes and other tobacco products are addicting, and nicotine is the drug that causes this addiction. "The physical and psychological processes that contribute to tobacco addiction are similar to those that cause heroin or cocaine addiction," the Surgeon General wrote. He believed tobacco is such a powerful drug that many teenage smokers are addicted by the time they reach young adulthood.

Addiction hard to break

Some alcoholics and hard drug users claim that their addiction to nicotine was harder to break than their addiction to alcohol and even to heroin. Most alcoholics can go without a drink longer than a heavy smoker can go without a cigarette. Even people who are being treated for severe smoking-related diseases may have trouble giving up cigarettes. Smokers who could not hold a cigarette in their lips because of mouth cancer have been reported to smoke cigarettes through breathing holes cut in their throats. Some patients with lung cancer continue to smoke despite their illness.

Besides nicotine, tar is another suspicious substance found in cigarette smoke. Tar is made up of hundreds of tiny particles. Many of these particles have been linked to disease. When they cool inside the lungs, they form a dark, sticky coating. This coating can damage the delicate lining in the lungs.

Research studies have linked tar to cancer, emphysema, and chronic bronchitis. Lung cancer can result when the lung cells begin to grow more rapidly than normal. Emphysema is a disease in which the lungs can no longer easily expand or contract. It cannot be cured. In chronic bronchitis, another tobacco-related disease, the airways leading to the lungs function poorly. They become narrow and lose their elasticity. Sticky mucus clogs the airways.

Besides tar and nicotine, cigarette smoke also contains carbon monoxide. This is the same odorless gas that is found in car exhaust fumes. It can be deadly in high doses. In the average cigarette, carbon monoxide makes up about 4 percent of the smoke. Carbon monoxide forces oxygen out of red blood cells. A healthy body needs a constant flow of oxygen.

In a heavy smoker, levels of carbon monoxide may be four to fifteen

---

☐ AIDS-related deaths: 8,959

☐ Homicides: 21,400

☐ Suicides: 31,470

☐ Motor-vehicle deaths: 48,560

Tobacco-related deaths: 350,000

The Risks of Smoking

Source: Centers for Disease Control, 1986 Figures.

times greater than those of a non-smoker. The gas may stay inside the body for up to six hours. Carbon monoxide is thought to make cholesterol build up inside blood vessels. Cholesterol is a fatty substance that coats the insides of arteries. Hardening of the arteries is a term used to describe heavy cholesterol deposits.

Smoking and heart disease

People commonly associate smoking with lung problems. What many do not realize is that smoking can damage the heart and blood vessels too. Most smoking-related deaths are not from lung cancer or emphysema, but from heart attacks. Smoking is a major cause of heart disease, according to many medical researchers.

When a person smokes, the heart must work harder to try to keep oxygen supplied to the body's cells. Blood pressure rises because nicotine causes blood vessels to become constricted. It takes more effort for the heart to pump blood through these constricted vessels. Also, carbon monoxide enters the bloodstream and replaces some of the oxygen. Body organs rely on oxygen to function properly, and when the oxygen level is constantly decreased, organ disease results.

The extra carbon monoxide may also damage the delicate linings of the arteries. Cholesterol may start to build up. Over time, these deposits get thicker and slow the flow of blood. When an artery leading to the heart becomes heavily blocked, a heart attack can occur. The American Heart Association warns that heavier smokers—those who smoke a pack a day—and people who adopt the smoking habit early in life run a greater risk of heart attack than non-smokers.

Heavy smokers also run the risk of having a stroke. A stroke occurs when the flow of blood and oxygen to the brain is cut off, injuring the brain. A stroke can paralyze parts of the body and destroy a person's ability to speak and remember things. Like heart attacks, strokes can be fatal. A full recovery is sometimes possible in the case of a milder stroke.

Chronic coughing, bronchitis, lung cancer, and emphysema can

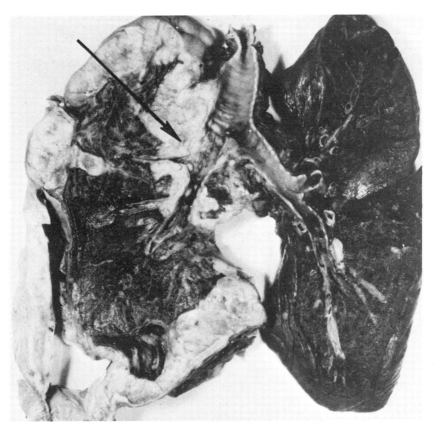

Inhaling the many irritants in cigarette smoke day after day, year after year, often results in lung cancer. The arrow in this photograph of a smoker's lungs points out one area of cancer in this diseased organ.

be traced to long-term cigarette smoking. The lungs of even new smokers are affected by smoking, though the damage may not be readily apparent. The ALA believes that teens who smoke regularly have more breathing and coughing problems than their non-smoking peers. Playing football or tennis, or dancing, may cause teenage smokers to tire more easily. This is because their lungs are not functioning to their full ability.

Smoking impairs the lungs' built-in ability to get rid of dirt and infections. Microscopic hairs, called cilia, line the inside of the lungs and sweep out irritants. Smoking can damage the cilia and cause them to slow down. When they cannot do their job, germs settle within the lungs. The risk of illness increases.

Chronic cough caused by smoking

Heavy smokers often develop a chronic cough. The chemicals in smoke irritate the lungs and airways. To clear the lungs, the natural response is to cough. Coughing helps the cilia to rid the lungs of tar and other chemicals. Even young smokers can develop a cough. The chronic cough could mean more serious problems, like emphysema, bronchitis, or even lung cancer.

Emphysema usually takes many years to develop. In this illness, the air sacs in the lungs lose their ability to force air in and out. Every breath becomes difficult. Emphysema patients can survive for many years with the help of oxygen tanks and special breathing exercises. Routine activities, like shopping, dancing, or washing the car, are difficult in the later stages of emphysema.

Bronchitis is another illness that affects smokers more than nonsmokers. The bronchi, or air tubes in the lungs, are also lined with cilia. Smoking slows their cleansing action and allows infections to develop. Coughing and fluid in the lungs are symptoms of bronchitis.

Besides bronchitis, the long-term heavy smoker runs the risk of lung cancer. The ALA states that cigarette smoking is the chief cause of lung cancer. This disease kills over eleven thousand people each year. Heavy smoking can destroy both the protective cilia and the air sacs in the lungs. If this happens, abnormal lung cells can grow and turn into cancer. Once lung cancer is discovered the cure rate is low. Only about 13 percent of lung cancer patients survive more than five years, according to the American Cancer Society (ACS).

The ACS recognizes that lung cancer is the nation's number one cancer among women. Some experts believe that this is the result of the smoking epidemic of the 1950s and 1960s. The ACS advises that the best defense against lung cancer is never to smoke or to quit smoking.

A healthy lung (left) has millions of flexible air sacs that can absorb oxygen from the breath. A lung with emphysema (right) loses much of this flexibility.

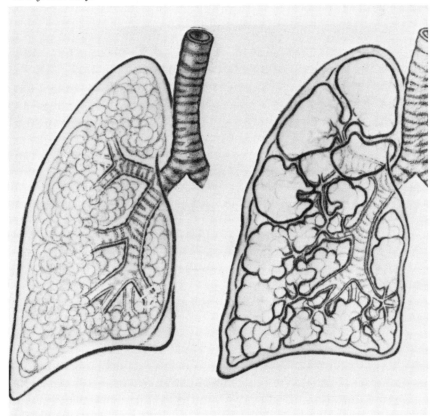

Evidence that smoking causes disease is mounting. But The Tobacco Institute denies that this evidence proves that smoking is linked to disease. In publications titled *The Cigarette Controversy*, and *Cigarette Smoking and Chronic Obstructive Lung Disease*, The Tobacco Institute defends itself.

Concerning the role smoking plays in heart disease, the Institute maintains that a causal relationship between smoking and heart disease has not been proved. More importantly, claims The Tobacco Institute, "no mechanism has been established to explain *how* tobacco smoke can cause CHD (chronic heart disease)."

To support this point, the Institute cites the findings of several scientific studies. For example, some studies show that ex-smokers have a lower rate of heart disease than those who have never smoked. Other studies done in Greece, Japan, and Finland show that smokers do not have a higher rate of heart disease than non-smokers. The Institute believes that there are many factors other than smoking that cause heart disease. These include pollution, alcohol use, and genetic factors. The Institute argues that past Surgeon Generals' reports have not adequately studied these causes.

Air pollution responsible for illness

The Tobacco Institute also denies that current evidence proves that smoking causes emphysema or bronchitis. The Institute claims that air pollutants have produced emphysema in lab animals, whereas similar studies with cigarette smoke have not.

As to the relationship between smoking and lung cancer, The Tobacco Institute claims that this disease may be linked to life-style, pollution in the workplace, and genetics rather than to smoking. For instance, people exposed to radon gas in their homes over a period of years could become victims of lung cancer. Radon is secreted from uranium deposits in the earth and is believed to cause lung cancer. Pollution in the workplace might also lead to lung cancer. People

who work with asbestos, a fire retardant, have high rates of lung cancer. Exposure to radiation on the job can also increase the risk of lung cancer.

According to The Tobacco Institute, lung cancer may also be a genetic disease. In other words, a certain family may be more likely to develop lung cancer than other families.

In defense of its products, The Tobacco Institute points out that most smokers do not get lung cancer. Among those who do, the cancer sometimes grows in a section of the lung that has been little exposed to smoke. Lung cancer rates are increasing among non-smokers, who also get the very same type of cancer that affects smokers. In view of these arguments, The Tobacco Institute maintains that it is difficult to blame lung cancer on smoking.

In fact, The Tobacco Institute denies that it has been proved that smoking causes any disease. The Institute wants more research into the causes of illnesses that have been blamed on smoking. The tobacco industry has already paid over 130 million dollars for research that was conducted by independent scientists. These scientists have produced almost twenty-six hundred publications on their findings. Despite these findings, The Tobacco Institute states that many unanswered questions about smoking and health still remain. According to the Institute, ''Science doesn't know the role, if any, smoking plays in the production of disease.''

Smoking and pregnancy

> A fervently wanted baby is born dead. The 34-year-old wife has smoked heavily throughout her pregnancy, and the infant's blood shows a nine-percent level of carboxyhemoglobin—from the smoke inhaled by the mother and transmitted into the fetal bloodstream, robbing it of vitally needed oxygen. This was equivalent to an incredible 41-percent decrease in the baby's blood flow during the mother's smoking hours.
> ''What Smoking Does to Women''
> By S.S. Field, *Reader's Digest*
> January 1976

Pregnant women risk the health of their unborn babies when they smoke. The chemicals a mother takes into her body from the smoke can affect the unborn child, or fetus. The ALA believes that smoking cuts down on the unborn baby's oxygen supply. Oxygen is needed to feed the baby's developing organs, including the lungs and the brain. The more a woman smokes while pregnant, the more she risks harming her baby's growth and health, according to many medical experts.

Some studies show that babies of smoking mothers tend to weigh less when they are born than babies born to non-smoking mothers.

Though extra weight is often gained after birth, the damage may already have been done. One study followed such children until they were seven years old. The children of smoking mothers remained shorter than their peers, could not read as well, and were not as well-adjusted.

Evidence also suggests that smoking during pregnancy can lead to an early delivery, a baby born with birth defects, a baby that is born dead—a still-birth, or a miscarriage. A miscarriage occurs in the early stages of pregnancy when the undeveloped baby, or fetus, is expelled from the body. Cigarette packages carry labels that warn pregnant women of these dangers.

Women over thirty-five who smoke and take birth control pills may also be at risk. Smoking and the pill can lead to blood vessel problems. A heart attack, stroke, or a blood clot may result. Any and all of these conditions can be deadly. A warning about mixing tobacco and birth control pills comes with the pills.

Besides contributing to disease and pregnancy complications, smoking may cause aging of the skin. Smoking has been blamed for premature facial wrinkles in both men and women. Healthy skin thrives on a constant supply of oxygen. Oxygen and nutrients flow through tiny blood vessels in the skin called capillaries. Smoking constricts capillaries at the same time as it replaces oxygen with carbon monoxide. Comparison studies show that after the age of thirty, heavy smokers, both men and women, were much more wrinkled than non-smokers.

Pipes, cigars, and smokeless tobacco

Cigar and pipe smokers tend to have lower death rates than cigarette smokers. But compared to the non-smoker, they have a higher death rate and are not as healthy. Cigar and pipe smoke contain many of the same harmful chemicals found in cigarette smoke. Fortunately, these smokers do not tend to inhale deeply and often smoke less than cigarette smokers.

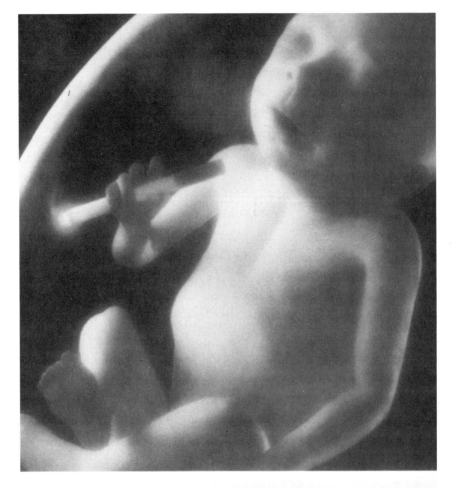

**WOULD YOU GIVE A CIGARETTE TO
YOUR UNBORN CHILD?**

YOU DO EVERY TIME YOU SMOKE!

A message from your doctor who is a member of the American College of
Obstetricians and Gynecologists and from the American Cancer Society.

Heart and lung diseases are less likely to strike pipe and cigar smokers. Instead, they are candidates for cancers of the mouth, lips, and larynx. The larynx is the ''voice box'' where sounds are made. These serious cancers can lead to disfigurement, loss of speech, and loss of life.

Those who smoke pipes and cigars face another problem. Their habit is generally unpopular in non-smoking circles. Many people find the odor of pipes and cigars unpleasant. These smokers may be asked to smoke outside, on the back porch, in the garage, or not at all.

Smokeless tobacco—chewing tobacco and snuff—solves the odor and smoke problems. But there are drawbacks there, too. One warning on a package of snuff reads, ''This product is not a safe alternative to cigarettes.'' Cancer of the lips, cheeks, gums, and throat has been linked to the use of smokeless tobacco.

Despite medical warnings, more young men are turning to these products each year. About 8-9 percent of men between the ages of seventeen and nineteen pinched snuff or chewed tobacco in 1986. Though far fewer in number, some women also do use these products.

Chewing tobacco consists of dried leaves that are chewed and spit out. Though containers called spittoons have been designed to catch this spit waste, chewers often spit wherever they happen to be—on city sidewalks, playgrounds, or ball fields. Older chewers can be recognized by their brown teeth and lips.

Snuff is made by grinding up tobacco. A pinch is usually placed between the lower lip and gums. Both snuff and chewing tobacco come in an assortment of appealing flavors, such as mint and cherry. Both are addictive and dangerous.

Passive smoking

Smokers are not the only ones who suffer from the side effects of smoke. Non-smokers in a smoke-filled room breathe many of the same toxic chemicals that the smoker does. The smoky irritants drifting off the end of a burning cigarette are even more poisonous than the drag the smoker inhales. These non-smokers are called passive smokers because they do not actively light up, yet their lungs and body become filled with smoke and chemicals.

Passive smokers can become ill as a result of cigarette smoke from others. Children of smokers have a greater risk of pneumonia, colds, and ear infections. The ability of their lungs to function may also be impaired. Parents who smoke in their children's presence run the risk of affecting their children's health.

Non-smoking spouses of heavy smokers may also be at risk. They

Many young people use smokeless tobacco products. No smoke means that others are not endangered by the product's use. But the user still risks cancer and addiction.

tend to suffer from more respiratory problems than the spouses of non-smokers. Some experts believe the non-smoking spouses of smokers also run an increased risk of lung cancer. Living in a smoke-filled environment for twenty or thirty years is bound to have a damaging effect on the non-smoker. If these experts are correct, the damage is far worse than most smokers ever suspected.

Where there's smoke, there's fire

Thousands of smoking-related fires occur each year. A small child plays with his big brother's matches and sets his room and himself ablaze. An older woman falls asleep with her favorite brand in hand. Smoke from her smoldering mattress smothers her in her sleep. A simmering cigar butt is tossed into the trash after a party. It ignites a living room. Millions of dollars worth of property and thousands of lives have been destroyed because of the careless use of matches and tobacco products.

Smoking takes its toll in a variety of ways. Poor health for countless active and passive smokers costs billions of dollars each year in medical treatment and research. Smokers are out sick from work and school more often than non-smokers. Costly delays in getting work done result when people are absent. Often someone else has to do extra duty.

CHAPTER SEVEN

How to Kick the Smoking Habit

Cigarette smoking can be costly and unhealthy. Cigarettes cost about 1.25 dollars per pack. Smokers spend millions of dollars each year on their addiction to nicotine. Smokers and their insurance companies paid over twenty-three billion dollars to treat medical problems related to smoking in 1984. Each year smoking costs U.S. society an estimated thirty-six billion dollars. Damage from fires, absences from work due to illness, and reduced job productivity are all parts of the equation that add up to this expensive total.

There are many benefits to be gained from giving up the smoking habit. People who no longer smoke can save their money to buy other things, like bikes, cars, and stereo equipment.

Ex-smokers and non-smokers do not have ''smoker's breath'' or yellow teeth. But they may have the experience of kissing a friend who does. Someone once said that kissing a smoker was like licking an ashtray.

Smokers who become ex-smokers have a greater chance of living healthier lives than do long-term smokers. Even young smokers who kick the habit feel better afterward. They usually find it easier to exercise, climb stairs, and dance the night away. Within twenty-four hours after a smoker takes the last puff, his or her body starts to rid itself of the poisonous substances built up from smoke—tar, nicotine, and carbon monoxide. The healing process begins right away.

As this healing process continues, quitters may experience withdrawal symptoms. Though these symptoms may cause discomfort and stress, they are signs that the body is getting back to normal. Dizziness can be a sign of withdrawal. This symptom may be the result of oxygen suddenly flowing to the brain instead of carbon monoxide. Arms and legs may tingle during the withdrawal phase. This happens because blood vessels have opened up, allowing blood to begin circulating normally to all parts of the body. Some new quitters complain of a hacking cough. This may be a signal that the cilia have gone back to work to sweep out tar deposits in the lungs. Within two to three weeks, most of these withdrawal symptoms disappear.

Withdrawal symptoms

Though withdrawal symptoms disappear in a relatively short period, the body requires more time to get back to normal. The amount of time the body needs to repair the damage depends on how long and how heavily a person has smoked. Smokers who have stopped in time may be able to reverse the damage done to their lungs, heart, and circulatory system. For the lucky ones, the risk of heart attack lessens after one year of abstinence. After ten years of non-smoking, the risk is about the same as for someone who has never smoked.

The withdrawal phase is a critical period for the would-be quitter. Because nicotine is such a powerful addicting substance, many smokers slip back into their old habits. An estimated 75 percent of all people who quit return to tobacco within a year. The body still craves nicotine. If a stressful event occurs or a situation in which one usually smoked arises, the ex-smoker may automatically reach for a cigarette.

Fighting nicotine addiction is hard. Even after smokers have a lung operation, heart surgery, or a heart attack, about half will still continue to smoke. Some smokers report that they have tried to give up cigarettes permanently for many years and failed. One technique, such as counseling, may work for a while, but the urge to smoke takes over again and again.

The good news is that over three million Americans win the battle against nicotine every year. Most successful ex-smokers try several times before they are able to break the habit. Most are unable to quit on the first or even second attempt. But the successful ones keep trying until they overcome their addiction. In spite of the setbacks, their commitment is stronger than the habit.

Most smokers who decide to quit go "cold turkey." They set a date to stop smoking for good. Some smokers quit gradually. This way is harder and leaves the door wide open to make excuses to have

"just one" or to smoke if something special happens. Smokers who go "cold turkey" have made up their minds for certain. They are more likely to become successful quitters than those who taper off.

Helpful tips for quitting

Depending on the method one selects, there are many helpful tips and approaches to kicking the habit:

• Involve a friend or family member. Get a buddy to give up the habit too. This person can provide support and a shoulder to lean on when temptation strikes. Help can be as near as the next room or a phone call away.

• Switch brands. Switch to a brand that tastes terrible. Enjoying it less will help you to smoke less. Some smokers change to a low tar and nicotine brand to wean themselves off cigarettes more gradually. This can work, as long as the smoker does not smoke more cigarettes and inhale more deeply to make up for the reduced nicotine intake.

• Break other habits that are associated with smoking. If coffee with a cigarette is the usual breakfast routine, take time to have cereal and toast instead. If smoking is a social pastime that is enjoyed with friends at a certain place, pass up these get-togethers for a few weeks until the withdrawal symptoms are gone and your willpower is stronger.

• Find oral substitutes. Smokers are used to having something in their mouths and hands. Keep toothpicks and sugarless gum handy. Some people chew cinnamon sticks that they can also handle like a cigarette.

• Eat a well-balanced diet. Many quitters report an increase in appetite and weight. Their taste buds have come alive again. To avoid the extra weight, quitters can carry a bag of raw vegetables with them for snacks. Drinking a glass of water before meals will help fill the stomach and trick the appetite into feeling satisfied. Daily exercise with well-balanced meals will also help keep unwanted pounds off.

Like other addictions, smoking can be difficult to give up. Most smokers do not succeed on their first attempt. But many stop-smoking methods and programs now exist to help them achieve their goal.

Gaining a few extra pounds may not be desirable, but it is less of a health threat than continued smoking.

• Join a stop smoking class or program. Health organizations, such as the American Lung Association and the American Cancer Society, sponsor classes to help smokers quit. Classes and clinics offered by these types of organizations are affordable and can be effective. The American Heart Association sponsors a special program for high school students. It is called Save a Sweetheart, or SASH. On Valentine's Day, young smokers take a pledge not to smoke. Their boyfriends and girlfriends encourage them to stay off cigarettes. The program is run by students and uses peer pressure to help smokers become confirmed non-smokers. Information on public programs and classes is free and can be obtained by calling the local offices of any of these organizations.

Commercial programs can also be helpful but are more expensive. Smokenders and the Schick Center offer well-known programs that can work.

• Get medical help. Some doctors put their patients on special programs to help them overcome the smoking habit. This may become essential after a heavy smoker has suffered a heart attack or stroke. Smoking then becomes a life-threatening habit. A medication called Nicorette may be given to some patients to help wean them from cigarettes. Nicorette is a gum that contains a little more nicotine than most cigarettes.

In spite of its benefits, some heavy users of Nicorette may get hooked on the gum. Because their bodies are still getting that old nicotine high they crave, some users chew constantly throughout the day. They may have simply traded one habit for another.

The smoking habit can be kicked. Smokers who want to quit must make the decision and recognize that they are capable of giving up tobacco products. Millions of people have thrown away their cigarettes, ashtrays, and lighters for good. Millions more will follow. But wouldn't it be easier to never even get started?

Glossary

addiction: a habit that is based on a physical and/or emotional dependence. Many smokers have a nicotine addiction.

archaeologist: a scientist who studies evidence of past cultures.

bronchitis: an inflammation of the airways, or bronchial tubes, that lead to the lungs. This inflammation causes the airways to narrow, lose their elasticity, or fill with fluid.

capillaries: tiny blood vessels that create a network throughout the body.

carbon monoxide: a colorless, odorless, tasteless gas that is poisonous. It is found in tobacco smoke.

cholesterol: fatty deposits that collect in and clog the lining of arteries and blood vessels. High cholesterol levels slow the flow of blood to vital organs. Smoking is believed to be a cause of cholesterol buildup.

cilia: tiny hair-like structures in the lungs. Through their swaying action, they sweep out irritating particles that collect in the lungs.

cold turkey: to stop an activity or give up a habit all at once. Some smokers go ''cold turkey'' to quit smoking.

emphysema: a disease associated with long-term smoking or breathing harmful irritants. As air sacs in the lungs lose their ability to force air in and out, it becomes harder for oxygen to enter the bloodstream.

epidemic: a rapid increase in the spread of a disease.

esophagus: the tube inside the throat that connects the pharynx with the stomach. The pharynx is a tube that connects the nasal cavity and mouth to the esophagus.

excise tax: a tax placed upon a product that is produced, sold, or used within a country.

fetus: an unborn baby that is not yet fully developed.

Nicorette: a chewing gum that contains nicotine. It is used to help people stop smoking by providing them the nicotine that their bodies crave.

nicotine: a naturally occurring poisonous drug found in tobacco.

passive smoking: the process of inhaling the smoke from other people's tobacco products. Passive smokers inhale a great deal of smoke that is not drawn through the cigarette or filtered through a smoker's lung. This unfiltered smoke contains a high degree of toxic substances, such as tar and nicotine.

snuff: finely ground tobacco. A "pinch" of snuff is usually placed in the cheek or under the lower lip.

stroke: a serious physical condition caused by lack of oxygen to the brain. When a blood vessel is clogged or bursts, vital nutrients cannot get to the brain. As a result, nerve cells in the affected area of the brain die.

tar: a coating of sticky smoke particles that collect inside the lung.

tariff: a tax on an imported or exported product.

withdrawal: physical and emotional changes caused by ceasing the use of a drug, such as nicotine or heroin. Withdrawal symptoms may include changes in heart rate, nervousness, and mood and sleep disturbances.

Organizations to Contact

Action on Smoking and Health
2013 H St. NW
Washington, D.C. 20006
(202) 659-4310

American Cancer Society
National Office
Tower Place
3340 Peachtree Road NE
Atlanta, Georgia 30026
(404) 320-3333

American Heart Association
National Center
7320 Greenville Ave.
Dallas, Texas 75231
(214) 750-5300

American Lung Association
1740 Broadway
New York, New York 10019
(212) 315-8700

Department of Agriculture
Agricultural Stabilization and Conservation Service
P.O. Box 2415
Washington, D.C. 20013
(202) 447-2567

The Great American Smokers Club, Inc.
P.O. Box 814206
Dallas, Texas 75381
(214) 386-8350

Hazelden Educational Materials
Pleasant Valley Road
Box 176
Center City, Minnesota 55012-0176
(800) 328-9000

National Institute on Drug Abuse
Department of Health and Human Services
5600 Fishers Lane
Rockville, Maryland 20857
(301) 468-2600

Smokers
P.O. Box 33602
Indianapolis, Indiana 42603
(317) PUFFERS

Technical Information Center
Office on Smoking and Health
U.S. Department of Health and Human Services
Park Building, Room 116
5600 Fishers Lane
Rockville, Maryland 20857
(301) 443-1690

The Tobacco Institute
1875 I St. NW
Washington, D.C. 20006
(202) 822-3393

Suggestions for Further Reading

Gilda Berger, *Smoking Not Allowed: The Debate.* New York: Franklin Watts, 1987.

Linda Bryson, *Are You Ready to Quit Smoking?* Dubuque, Iowa: Kendall/Hunt, 1983.

Dee Burton and Gary Wohl, *The Joy of Quitting—How to Help Young People Stop Smoking.* New York: Collier Books, 1979.

Curtis W. Casewit, *Quit Smoking.* Rockport, Massachusetts: Para Research, 1983.

Claudia Bialke Debner, ed., *Chemical Dependency.* St. Paul, Minnesota: Greenhaven Press, 1985.

Nancy R. Gibbs, "All Fired Up Over Smoking," *Time*, April 18, 1988.

Richard Lacayo, "Smoke Gets in Your Rights," *Time*, April 18, 1988.

Margaret McKean, *The Stop Smoking Book.* San Luis Obispo, California: Impact Publications, 1987.

David Owen, "The Cigarette Companies: How They Get Away with Murder," *Washington Monthly*, March 1985.

Brooke Shields, *On your Own.* New York: Villard Books, 1985.

Susan Wagner, *Cigarette Country.* New York: Praeger, 1971.

The Tobacco Institute, *The Cigarette Controversy: Why More Research Is Needed.* Washington, D.C.: The Tobacco Institute, 1984.

Index

Picture Credits

Cover Photo: American Cancer Society

American Cancer Society, 26, 52, 65, 67, 72, 74, 80

American Cancer Society and J. Walter Thompson advertising agency, 24

American Lung Association, 35

Tony Auth. Copyright 1987, Universal Press Syndicate. Reprinted with permission. All rights reserved, 19

Steve Benson. Reprinted by permission: Tribune Media Services, 32

Berke Breathed. © 1988, Washington Post Writers Group. Reprinted with permission, 47

Culver Pictures, 12, 15, 30

Mike Keefe. Reprinted with permission, 13

Steve Kelley. Reprinted with permission, 69

Jeff MacNelly. Reprinted by permission: Tribune Media Services, 78

Northwest Airlines and Saatchi & Saatchi DFS Compton Inc., 59

Steve Sack. Reprinted by permission of the *Star Tribune*, 27

John Trever. Reprinted with permission, 55

Reprinted with permission: Tribune Media Services, 54

United States Department of Agriculture, 41, 44

United States Public Health Service, Office of the Surgeon General, 20

About the Author

Lila Gano is a technical writer and analyst with a defense contractor in Chula Vista, California. She writes reports and computer-use manuals. In addition, she has had several articles published in her company's monthly news magazine.

Ms. Gano received her bachelor's degree in sociology and anthropology and her master's degree in psychology and counseling. As an officer in the Navy, she conducted an evaluation of the Navy's substance abuse programs. She also supervised an evaluation of fifty-five youth employment programs for high school dropouts.

Ms. Gano lives on a 42-foot power boat near San Diego, California.